NARROW WAY

KEN DOSS

CONTENTS

Preface: About This Book iii

1 The Narrow Way 4
2 Heaven or Hell? 13
3 God is Love 19
4 The Way 27
5 The Truth 32
6 The Life 40
7 Born Again 49
8 Jesus is Lord and Savior 55
9 Dad and Son 61

PREFACE

ABOUT THIS BOOK

The purpose of this book is simple. My hope and prayer is that everyone who reads this book comes to know Jesus better. If you don't know Him personally, my prayer is that you come to know Him in a close personal way as your Lord and Savior. If you know Him my prayer is that you get to know Him better. Jesus loves you and wants you to have eternal life with Him.

Chapters 1 through 8 are conversations between a Pastor and a member of his church. Chapter 9 is a conversation between myself and my son.

CHAPTER 1

THE NARROW WAY

BROTHER: Pastor, the Holy Spirit has shown me something.

PASTOR: What's that?

BROTHER: I was reading Matthew and something jumped out at me.

PASTOR: Go on.

BROTHER: Let me read this to you, Matthew 7:13-23:

> "Enter by the narrow gate; for wide is the gate and broad is the way that leads to destruction, and there are many who go in by it. Because narrow is the gate and difficult is the way which leads to life, and there are few who find it."
>
> "Beware of false prophets who come to you in sheep's clothing, but inwardly they are ravenous wolves. You will know them by their fruits. Do men gather grapes from thornbushes or figs from thistles?"
>
> "Even so, every good tree bears good fruit, but a bad tree bears bad fruit. A good tree cannot bear bad fruit, nor can a bad tree bear good fruit. Every tree that does not bear good fruit is cut down and thrown into the fire. Therefore by their fruits you will know them."
>
> "Not everyone who says to Me, 'Lord, Lord,' shall enter the kingdom of heaven, but he who does the will of My Father in heaven. Many will say to Me in that day, Lord, Lord, have we not prophesied in Your name, and done many wonders in Your name? And then I will declare to them, 'I never knew you; depart from Me, you who practice lawlessness!'"

BROTHER: When I read this the word MANY jumped out at me twice. First, many go the broad way that leads to destruction and then Jesus says. *"Many will say to Me in that day, Lord, Lord, have we not prophesied in Your name, and done many wonders in Your name?"* And he says to them, *'I never knew you; depart from Me, you who practice lawlessness!*

PASTOR: There are many things that jump out. Many will go on the broad path of destruction. I think they're being deceived. What do you think?

BROTHER: The thing that jumps out at me is in the beginning, where it says that many go the way of destruction, but few go the narrow way. Then you drop down and Jesus says, *"Many will say to Me in that day, Lord, Lord',* And he says to them, *'I never knew you; depart from Me, you who practice lawlessness!"*
   I ask you, have you ever heard this preached? Are people even aware this is in there? Sounds like church people to me. I don't know, you tell me.

PASTOR: I think many people come to church on Sunday and think they've completed some sort of religious obligation by their attendance and that puts them on the narrow path, but in reality if they're not following the teachings and ideals of Jesus in their lives they could very well be on the broad path that leads to destruction, and if their pastors are not clearly pointing to Jesus as the answer they may themselves be on that broad path to destruction.

BROTHER: So have you ever preached this section of scripture to the church?

PASTOR: Yes I have brother, and I'm pretty sorry you asked, because as I recall you were sitting in the second row asleep.

BROTHER: I could have been. Lord forgive me if I was.

There's hearty laughter between the two.

BROTHER: Now we're at a point where we both see clearly the church in general has gotten away from what Jesus wants us to be about. This is a strong warning directly from Jesus. I don't see how we can take this lightly. It's really to the point.

PASTOR: One of the things we should probably look at besides the many is the few who enter by the narrow gate. Jesus says, *"Because narrow is the gate and difficult is the way which leads to life, and there are few who find it."* So we need to know what qualifies one to enter by the narrow gate.

BROTHER: Is it possible most of the people sitting here in church on Sunday are not even aware of this? That they are part of the many? Is that what you are saying?

PASTOR: Sad to say, but I think that's the reality in this day and age. Very few people want to be confronted by the words of Jesus.

BROTHER: So how do we help change this? Neither one of us want to see all these people stand before the Lord on that day and not be known by Him. What is it that people have to do to be known by Him?

PASTOR: I think a person needs to know if they're on that broad path. The first requirement of getting off that path is repentance and acknowledging their shortcomings of not walking in the statutes the Lord has given us. Jesus says the many are practicing lawlessness.

BROTHER: Most of what I remember in my church years is being encouraged to accept Jesus as our Lord and Savior. A lot of these people are going to confess that they've done that. Isn't that enough?

PASTOR: It's not enough to proclaim Jesus as Lord and Savior and then not do what he says. Jesus said *"If you love Me, keep My commandments."* (John 14:15) The reality is if we don't walk in His statutes and we add some traditions of men that eliminate part of His statutes, He's not going to find that acceptable. Those are some of the people that are on the broad path.

BROTHER: Doesn't this somehow have to be simple? Doesn't He somewhere say that we need to come to Him as little children and believe? (Matthew 18:3)

PASTOR: I think the simplicity has been lost. In its simplest form it's about loving God and loving your neighbor as yourself. It's about allowing the character of Christ to blossom in one's life and not walking according to the traditions of men, but walking according to the commands of God.

BROTHER: Isn't it even deeper than that in the sense that, I mean, He says right here He doesn't know these people, so doesn't that mean that we have to know Him personally. There has to be a connection, a relationship with Him.

PASTOR: Taking a step back, loving God with your whole heart, mind, soul and strength you're going to develop relationship with Him through prayer, through obedience, through . . .

BROTHER: Through Love . . . Through Love.

PASTOR: Through Love. Jesus said, *"You shall love the Lord your God with all your heart, with all your soul, and with all your mind. This is the first and great commandment. And the second is like it: You shall love your neighbor as yourself. On these two commandments hang all the Law and the Prophets."* (Matthew 22:37-40). He didn't say pretend like we do, He said to do. There is a difference. It's a heart change. It's an inward change to an outward stimulus. We love those around us and we love God in Heaven. We live lives of love.

BROTHER: So how in the world did we get so distracted? How did the church get like this?

PASTOR: I think a lot of it came about by hoping a two minute prayer is the ticket to heaven and a fire escape from hell. A two minute prayer is the down payment. If there's no presence of the Lord in one's life he or she needs to examine things, and pray for the Holy Spirit to show them the truth.

BROTHER: In other words that two minute prayer may just be when someone knocked on the door, the door opened, but they didn't walk through.

PASTOR: Oh yea, it's a very straight narrow way, it's not easy, it's not crowded, because you have to lay down your life and pick up His cross and follow Him. He said His commandments are not strenuous or burdensome. People have come to a place where they think they are. It's just not so. It's only burdensome if you disagree with God. He says 'don't sin' and you say 'but I want to'. Suddenly it became a burden. Do you remember this? Jesus says, *"Take My yoke upon you and learn from Me, for I am gentle and lowly in heart, and you will find rest for your souls. For My yoke is easy and My burden is light."* (Matthew 11:29-30)

BROTHER: So you're saying it's possible that a lot of people went forward in church and said that two minute prayer and accepted Jesus, and somehow they were thinking it was a fire escape from hell, and yet it didn't settle with them or it didn't take to the point that it became the core of their being.

PASTOR: I think a lot of preaching, in fact churches have been built on the idea or misconception that grace covers sin. If there's intentional sin in your life, you probably want to examine if you're really saved or not. If you're truly born again into the kingdom of God it should be your good will to do the will of God the Father. If it's not, then there's something that needs some serious examination. If one is unwilling to do this, they're probably not where they need to be or where God wants them. A lot of churches, even mega churches don't preach against sin or how to live in the will of God. They have a very liberal viewpoint, almost like an intangible socially correct dogma that's a lie. Jesus made it so simple, He said *"If you love Me, keep My commandments."* (John 14:15)

BROTHER: Maybe part of what's going on is that we were literally bought with a price by what Jesus did on the cross, a sacrifice for our sins. We are no longer our own. He wants to be our Lord. He wants to be in control and for a lot of us that's a battle. If we have asked Him to be our Lord and Savior and then ignore Him aren't we back on that broad path that leads to destruction? I think His presence and guidance and love are on the narrow path.

PASTOR: He is the Lord. I personally don't want to be in a position where I acknowledge Him as my Lord and then try to live without his guidance every day of my life. This isn't being preached in the churches in a way that confronts the truth.

BROTHER: I'd guess if this is preached, a lot of people are going to take offense. They don't want the control of their lives examined by anyone. It seems like the big churches are often full because the people are being fed a menu of self congratulations and justification to live in a way that fulfills them and makes them feel good or maybe just acceptable to each other.

PASTOR: People need to be informed about what He requires to be saved. The truth is we need to keep His words and keep the commandments. We do need to confess Him as our Lord and Savior and then we need to allow Him to be our Lord and Savior.

If we love Him we will find ourselves hungering for His presence in our prayers. We will find His love, wisdom, and guidance by reading His words in the gospels, by knowing and keeping His commandments. His peace can be upon us when we are walking on the straight and narrow path.

BROTHER: You can't earn your way into heaven, and yet at the same time if there's no evidence of Jesus in your life then somehow you may not be where you think you are.

PASTOR: The reality is that Jesus said the world will know that the Father sent the Son because of the love you have for one another. And so if you want the world to see that the Father sent the Son, you need to love one another. The truth is that if we loved one another the way Jesus prescribed, then the world would see that the Father sent the Son.

BROTHER: I get that, but again how does anyone, let alone a preacher get the truth out there in a way that's going to get through to people?

PASTOR: First of all I believe it is only the Holy Spirit that can draw people to the truth. He can work through a preacher or anyone else who has submitted themselves to Christ. Prayer is a key ingredient. When we agree with the Father about His desire that none should perish, no not one, and then let the Holy Spirit guide us, the message can flow out.

BROTHER: I will be in prayer about all this and I'll ask Him to bless you and anoint you like never before.

PASTOR: I truly appreciate your prayers. We should spend more time in joint prayer.

BROTHER: I agree.

PASTOR: I've been praying about a sermon close to what we've been talking about and part of it might be this verse out of Philippians. Verse 2:12, this is Paul writing to the Philippians, he says, *"Therefore, my beloved, as you have always obeyed, not as in my presence only, but now much more in my absence, work out your own salvation with fear and trembling."* I would stress the phrase, 'WORK OUT YOUR OWN SALVATION WITH FEAR AND TREMBLING'.

BROTHER: That's powerful.

PASTOR: I know. I wonder how it'll be received.

There is an uncomfortable moment of silence.

BROTHER: Are you asking me?

PASTOR: Yea. What's your take?

BROTHER: My opinion probably shouldn't matter. I would encourage you to pray about it until you have peace about it.

PASTOR: You got a few minutes?

BROTHER: Sure.

PASTOR: Let me read this to you, Revelation, Chapter 21: *"Now I saw a new heaven and a new earth, for the first heaven and the first earth had passed away. Also there was no more sea."*

"Then I, John, saw the holy city, New Jerusalem, coming down out of the heaven from God, prepared as a bride adorned for her husband."

"And I heard a loud voice from heaven saying, "Behold, the tabernacle of God is with men, and He will dwell with them, and they shall be His people. God Himself will be with them and be their God."

"And God will wipe away every tear from their eyes; there shall be no more death, nor sorrow, nor crying. There shall be no more pain, for the former things have passed away."

"Then He who sat on the throne said, "Behold, I make all things new." And He said to me, "Write, for these words are true and faithful."

"And He said to me, "It is done! I am the Alpha and the Omega, the Beginning and the End. I will give of the fountain of the water of life freely to him who thirsts."

"He who overcomes shall inherit all things, and I will be his God and he shall be My son."

"But the cowardly, unbelieving, abominable, murderers, sexually immoral, sorcerers, idolaters, and all liars shall have their part in the lake which burns with fire and brimstone, which is the second death."

BROTHER: It's powerful.

PASTOR: This is part of what the Holy Spirit is pouring out on me. I believe everyone needs to hear this, read this, repeatedly, if necessary, pray about it, and then work out their salvation with fear and trembling.

Let's Pray!

CHAPTER 2

HEAVEN OR HELL?

PASTOR: Hello brother.

BROTHER: What's going on?

PASTOR: You look a little bothered by something. You got something on your mind?

BROTHER: I'm not sure I can talk about it.

PASTOR: Try me. You never know.

BROTHER: The Lord's shown me something I don't think people want to hear. I was reading Matthew yesterday and I read through most of it. I never realized before how much Jesus talks about heaven and hell. Yesterday it seemed like the theme of what the Holy Spirit wanted me to see is that heaven and hell are real, and each of us is going to one or the other. There aren't any alternatives. I'm not sure most people really comprehend this reality.

PASTOR: Jesus makes it extremely obvious that there is heaven and there is hell. He also makes it obvious that we're going to one or the other. He gives us guidelines to live by to help us secure heaven and if we walk outside those guidelines we can be in danger of hell. We're looking at eternity here, no end. For some reason people tend to skip over heaven and hell to focus on what they consider good parts.

BROTHER: It seems like people don't grasp that Jesus says hell is fire, it's eternal torment, it's a place where the worm turns for eternity. Eternity is something that is real hard to get a hold of.

BROTHER: On the other hand heaven is actually a place where you can be in Gods presence, where there is love beyond our imagination. We probably can't even get close to understanding how fabulous it's going to be. He promised that He's going to His Fathers house where there are many mansions. A place where there's no more tears, not more pain and suffering. It seems like people aren't delighting in being able to have that possibility, that reality.

PASTOR: I think you're exactly right. I think they neglect to see that the escape from hell is through repentance. One of the first things Jesus spoke to the people about is repentance. The word shows that the fruit of repentance is turning to Him and following Him. His promise to us, if we follow Him is that we're going to be fishers of men. It sounds like work, but if you're truly in Christ Jesus, it becomes your good pleasure to do what He wants. That's the escape from the eternal damnation, hellfire, brimstone, and torment.

BROTHER: And separation from God.

PASTOR: Perhaps that's exactly what it is. Having a personal relationship with Jesus, seeking His Lordship in our lives and walking is His commandments can insure our entry into heaven. He can't be fooled. He knows what's going on. Walking outside His truth insures an eternity in hell. Jesus said *"If you love Me, keep My commandments."* (John 14:15). He also said *"But why do you call Me Lord, Lord' and not do the things I say?"* (Luke 6:46) If we want to go to heaven we need to do what He says. Heaven and hell are real places, there's no doubt about it. Our final destination depends on how we walk out our relationship with Him.

BROTHER: Jesus said, *"But seek first the kingdom of God and His righteousness, and all these things shall be added to you."* (Matthew 6:33) He's giving us instruction there, to seek His kingdom first and His righteousness and then all things will be added to us.

PASTOR: Too many times, we make this more complicated than it really is. We need to seek the Lord constantly, truly allowing Him to be our Master. Through prayer, and letting His words and commandments live inside us with the help of the Holy Spirit, He can enable us to overcome the desires of our flesh and the temptations this world has to offer. When we mess up we can go to Him and confess our sin and weakness. He is quick to forgive us if our repentance is genuine. We can't trick Him. He knows us better than we know ourselves. It can become our good pleasure to please God. This is a new way of life. I don't think it's a single event. If the two minute prayer is all people are trusting in to keep them out of Hell, I fear for them.

BROTHER: So it would appear that through the process of really having a relationship with Christ, and allowing Him to rule and reign in our lives, He wants to continue to purify us and prepare us for what is ahead of us. It still puzzles me why people don't have a sense, and I'm not saying all people, but a lot of people don't have a sense that eternity is going to go on forever and at some point you're going to find yourself in one place or the other, heaven or hell. It's serious stuff and people don't take it serious.

PASTOR: It is a walk. It's a walk from the first day you say you need a Savior, to the last day you're here. Each day you walk in the truth of the living God you grow closer to Him. Jesus said, *"Ask, and it will be given to you; seek, and you will find, knock, and it will be opened to you."* (Matthew 7:7) One of the things encompassed in this scripture is that seeking Him is a process that lasts the rest of our lives, and as we continue to seek we continue to find. It doesn't mean at some point . . ."

BROTHER: You think you've arrived?

PASTOR: Yea. It doesn't stop because you said, 'Jesus come into my life.' It starts when you say, 'Jesus come into my life.' You'll find so much depth, knowledge and understanding if you continue to seek God. When I look at a lot of the church I see people who don't seek and they've stopped right where they are. Does that mean they're escaping hell or making it to heaven? I don't know. God's the judge. There isn't any denying that the Heavenly Father and Jesus want us to keep the commandments. So if we seek the will of the Father, have a prayer life, seek and obey the guidance of the Holy Spirit in our life we're where He wants us to be. I know it can't be done without Him. If you try to live by the law, by the commandments without Him, in your own strength and flesh it won't work. That's what the Pharisees were trying to do. Read chapter 23 of Matthew. Jesus pours out the truth about the works of the Pharisees. God wants to change us from the inside out, not from the outside in.

BROTHER: Oh man, let me read this scripture, maybe it well help. Jesus says, *"Then the King will say to those on His right hand, 'Come, you blessed of My Father, inherit the kingdom prepared for you from the foundation of the world; for I was hungry and you gave Me food; I was thirsty and you gave Me drink; I was a stranger and you took Me in; 'I was naked and you clothed Me; I was sick and you visited Me; I was in prison and you came to Me.*
"Then the righteous will answer Him, saying, 'Lord, when did we see You hungry and feed You, or thirsty and give You drink? 'When did we see You a stranger and take You in, or naked and clothe You? 'Or when did we see You sick, or in prison, and come to You?'"
"And the King will answer and say to them, "Assuredly, I say to you, inasmuch as you did it to one of the least of these My brethren, you did it to Me."
"Then He will also say to those on the left hand, 'Depart from Me, you cursed, into the everlasting fire prepared for the devil and his

angels; 'for I was hungry and you gave Me no food; I was thirsty and you gave Me no drink'; 'I was a stranger and you did not take me in, naked and you did not clothe Me, sick and in prison and you did not visit Me.'"

"Then they also will answer Him, saying, 'Lord when did we see You hungry or thirsty or a stranger or naked or sick or in prison, and did not minister to You?"

"Then He will answer them, saying, 'Assuredly, I say to you, inasmuch as you did not do it to one of the least of these, you did not do it to Me.'"

"And these will go away into everlasting punishment, but the righteous into eternal life." (Matthew 25:34-46)

This scripture tells me clearly, there's a distinction, some are going to heaven for eternity and some are going to hell for eternity. He knows who is with Him and who is against Him.

PASTOR: That's a great point. One of the things in there is the righteous asking the King, *'when did we do these things?'* And he basically tells them that when they do things to help others in need they are doing His will and they will be rewarded. Eternity in the kingdom, eternity in heaven awaits them. I think a lot of people who are in Christ, do good things, without really paying attention to each incident, because the nature of Christ comes out of them, sometimes without them thinking about it. It's not a work for them, it's simply who they are.

BROTHER: It's an opportunity for Him to work through us, and in the process we grow closer to Him and let Him become a bigger part of who we are.

PASTOR: And on the other hand you have goats. They may have had what the people needed, but wouldn't give it to them. They kept it for themselves or maybe thought by giving to some big TV ministry they'd be rewarded more than they gave. Some of these ministries are living in mansions and yet there's a world out there where people are living in cardboard boxes. It's a matter of the heart. God knows what's in everyone's heart. He knows who is with Him and who is against Him. It really is simple, seek Him, love Him, let Him be your Lord and Savior, do His will and eternity with Him in heaven is yours. Or you can ignore Him, or pretend to know Him, live your life selfishly, and eternity in hell, with everlasting fire awaits you. It doesn't seem like a hard choice, but for those who are hell bound I can't believe that they know where they're headed.

BROTHER: Christ died for us. He wants us to accept what He did on the cross for each of us personally. He wants to live inside our hearts. He wants to rule and reign in our lives, to guide us and direct us in all things. He doesn't want us to go to hell. He wants us to spend eternity in heaven with Him and the Father. It makes me think of the line out of an old hymn, "What a day of rejoicing it will be."

PASTOR: Well said. I wish I could get everyone to read all of 1 John. 1 John 2:15-17 says: *"Do not love the world or the things in the world. If anyone loves the world, the love of the Father is not in him. For all that is in the world – the lust of the flesh, the lust of the eyes, and the pride of life – is not of the Father but is of the world. And the world is passing away, and the lust of it; but he who does the will of God abides forever."*

BROTHER: Wow. That's blunt. Maybe the way to share this with people is to simply read all these scriptures to them, slowly, and stop now and then, for prayer. Invite the Holy Spirit to join us and delight in us.

PASTOR: You might have something there. Let's pray.

CHAPTER 3

GOD IS LOVE

PASTOR: Hey Bro, how you doing? What's going on?

BROTHER: I'm doing good. I had a conversation with Ray the other day at work. It was pretty cool. He was gone last week on vacation. He took his family to Universal Studios Theme Park in southern California. He told me when he was over there he was impressed with how many people are in the Los Angeles basin, thousands upon thousands, literally millions of people. He said he got this understanding of how God knows about each of these people, how many hairs on each one of their heads, and He knows more about the depths of each person than they know about themselves. It opened the door for me to talk to him about how much God loves everybody. God is not like us. He is majestic. He is bigger and broader than any of us have a clue about, and yet He loves each one of us individually, more than we can even begin to comprehend. It was a good thing.

PASTOR: There's no question God loves us. The bigger question is how well do we know ourselves? Not as well as God knows us.

BROTHER: One of the things we talked about is the realization that as individuals we are like microscopic specks on this planet and yet God loves each one of us and each one of us is very special to Him. There's over 7 billion people on this planet and yet God knows each and every one of them in such detail that we never begin to comprehend. I told Ray, if you can get your mind around that, and then realize the Earth is just a minute speck in the galaxy, and the galaxy is a speck in the universe. Wow! Yet the God that created and sustains all of this loves each of us. He wants to be connected to each of us in love and have a relationship with each of us that grows and flourishes. In the creation process it says that we were made in His image, so to God each one of us is unique and very special. He loves us, way beyond our comprehension. In the big scheme of things His ultimate desire is to have an intimate personal relationship with each of us. This started in the Garden of Eden with Adam and Eve. He wanted a relationship with them and today He's after a relationship with us. I was able to share this with Ray and my hope and prayer is that God is drawing on his heart and bringing him into the truth.

PASTOR: I hope and pray the same thing.

BROTHER: If you had the opportunity to tell Ray about Gods love, what would you tell him?

PASTOR: God created the heavens and earth and everything in them, on them, above them and below them. He created us to have a relationship with Him, and it's not to get to know us, He already knows us better than we know ourselves. He loves us and wants us to know Him, to love Him, to trust Him, and get to a place where we are in awe of Him, and worship Him to the core of our hearts and souls. God has shown us over and over again how we can walk with Him in love and have a relationship with Him. Let me read this to you, 1 John 4:7-8 reads:

"Beloved, let us love one another, for love is of God; and everyone who loves is born of God and knows God. He who does not love does not know God, for God is love."

Let me repeat. God is love.

BROTHER: Very true.

PASTOR: Another thing I pray everyone would understand, there is an enemy, an adversary that is hell bent on keeping us separated from the love of God. Satan will use anything he can to keep us from the truths about God. Satan will use friends, family, pride, puffed up intellect, or supposed intellect, lust, even religion, churches, pastors, priests if he can get away with it. Satan's desire is to destroy each of us by whatever means possible.

How many people are deceived or at the least robbed of the fullness of their relationship with God, because they've been spoon fed a verse or two and place their faith in a holding pattern?

John 3:16 says, *"For God so loved the world that He gave His only begotten Son, that whoever believes in Him should not perish but have everlasting life."*

Now let me read John 3:16-21;

"For God so loved the world that He gave His only begotten Son, that whoever believes in Him should not perish but have everlasting life."

"For God did not send His Son into the world to condemn the world, but that the world through Him might be saved."

"He who believes in Him is not condemned; but he who does not believe is condemned already, because he has not believed in the name of the only begotten Son of God."

"And this is the condemnation, that the light has come into the world, and men loved darkness rather than light, because their deeds were evil."

"For everyone practicing evil hates the light and does not come to the light, lest his deeds should be exposed."

"But he who does the truth comes to the light, that his deeds may be clearly seen; that they have been done in God."

I know that is some deep scripture to process, but I think you get the point. Hanging your faith, your life on one cherry picked verse could be eternally disastrous. See what I'm saying?

BROTHER: Yes.

PASTOR: The precious thing to God is the relationship between Him and us, and Satan wants to destroy it. He wants to prohibit it, inhibit it, he wants to stop it in any way he can. God's word says that Satan's purpose is to rob, steal and destroy, to interrupt a relationship with God. Satan uses everything that God created, or that man created to separate man from God, from Gods love. He uses a lot of processes to do this. One of the processes is religion. False religions that explain to people that there is another way to heaven other than what Gods Word says, something different than *"For God so loved the world that He gave His only begotten Son, that whoever believes in Him should not perish but have everlasting life."*

God the Father loved what he created and he gave His only begotten Son to reestablish a relationship with us.

BROTHER: This is what I was trying to get across to Ray, God wants to have a relationship with us, it's the desire of His heart. God loves us and He wants us to love Him. It appears that a lot of what goes on in some churches is a distraction from that. Somehow it distracts or impedes people from having a deep personal relationship with God. It's not something that's controlled by a church or a pastor or a priest. Go back to Matthew 7:22-23 Jesus says. *"Many will say to Me in that day, Lord, Lord, have we not prophesied in Your name, and done many wonders in Your name?" And then I will declare to them, 'I never knew you; depart from Me, you who practice lawlessness!"*

Think about what He's saying there. *'I never knew you.'* It's crystal clear to me, He wants to know us personally. It's not something you can ride on the coat tails of your grandparents or parents because they were churchgoers. It means you have to establish a relationship with Him, and the only way I know to do that is through Christ Jesus.

PASTOR: You're absolutely correct, which brings me to another place. The relationship can't be made for you. The church can't have the relationship for you. The priest can't have the relationship for you. The pastor can't have the relationship for you. Your dad can't and your mom can't. You have to have that relationship yourself. Jesus opens a way for us to have dialogue or pray with the Father. John 14:6 reads:

"Jesus said to him, I am the way, the truth, and the life. No one comes to the Father except through Me."

So we can have a relationship with the Father through Jesus Christ in prayer. How can we get there through Jesus? Jesus is that propitiation for us. Jesus is an advocate for us. The Father can't look on sin. He loved us enough to give His Son so that through the blood of Christ we can have a relationship with the Father. Nobody can have that relationship for you. Hopefully those who teach you encourage you to have that personal relationship, instead of teaching you to attempt a relationship through religion, or works. You can only have a relationship with the Father through faith in Jesus Christ.

God is all knowing, perfect, righteous, and Holy. He can't have a relationship with unholy beings like us. We needed a way to Him, because we are not worthy in and of ourselves. In the old testament times there was a system of animal blood sacrifices, but it was not adequate. The blood of a perfect Savior, Jesus, is adequate. I don't know a better way to put it, all the things we're talking about tell us God the Father loves us beyond measure and was willing to sacrifice His only begotten Son to make a way for us to have a relationship with Him and receive Him and His love into our hearts.

BROTHER: The Holy Spirit has repeatedly lead me to share the conversation between Nicodemus and Jesus with Ray. John 3:1-7 reads:
"There was a man of the Pharisees named Nicodemus, a ruler of the Jews. This man came to Jesus by night and said to Him, "Rabbi, we know that You are a teacher come from God; for no one can do these signs that You do unless God is with him."

> *Jesus answered and said to him, "Most assuredly, I say to you, unless one is born again, he cannot see the kingdom of God."*
>
> *Nicodemus said to Him, "How can a man be born when he is old? Can he enter a second time into his mother's womb and be born?"*
>
> *Jesus answered, "Most assuredly, I say to you, unless one is born of water and the Spirit, he cannot enter the kingdom of God.*
>
> *That which is born of the flesh is flesh, and that which is born of the Spirit is spirit.*
>
> *Do not marvel that I said to you, "You must be born again."*

I hope it was clear to Ray that we must be born again to even see the kingdom of God, let alone enter the kingdom of God. And I hope and pray that the Holy Spirit will clearly reveal to Ray that believing in and receiving Jesus Christ as Lord and Savior, is the door to the kingdom of God. It is the beginning of a personal relationship with God the Father through His one and only Son, Jesus.

PASTOR: I hope and pray the same thing.

BROTHER: Once you've walked through the door, which is Jesus, it's just the beginning of your relationship with God the Father. It's a lot like any relationship we have. We have to spend time with someone to get to know them, and the more time we spend the more our relationship grows and flourishes. I believe God wants us to walk through the door and get to know Him and continue on in a relationship that is deep, and grows through eternity.

PASTOR: In that is the love of God towards man. There is no other thing I can think of to build on it. We both have sons, I don't know about you, but I can't imagine giving my son to save some low life individual, like myself. It's just about impossible to grasp the depth of God's love for us. It humbles me when I focus on it. My eyes swell with tears as I dwell on it. To know that we can be right with the Father through the precious blood of Jesus is almost unfathomable.

BROTHER: I know what you're saying.

PASTOR: I have this burning desire to help people to understand that our relationship with God can't become stagnant, it has to keep moving like running water. You know what happens when water stands?

BROTHER: It can grow bad stuff and become unfit.

PASTOR: Exactly. If we ever reach a place where we think we have arrived, we need to ask the Father for help in the name of Jesus. Things have been lost in the translation of languages. In Matthew 6:33 Jesus says: *"But seek first the kingdom of God and His righteousness, and all these things shall be added to you."*
Part of the meaning of the word seek in the original language is to continue to seek, and seek, and seek, and seek. The seeking should never stop.

BROTHER: One of the remarkable things about having a relationship with Him, is He will give you insight and truth that is not available in the world. He can get you to a point where you realize He knows what's best for you and yet part of what we're being taught in this culture is that everything should be about us and our desires, our pleasures, and our self fulfillment. According to much of the world it's all about being self centered, which is really another definition for selfishness. Yet once you come to know Him, and receive His love, and let some of His peace be upon you it becomes clear that this world and everything in it is temporary. This world and everything in it is going to be destroyed and eternity is what really matters. It's hard to get your mind around eternity, but you certainly want to be on the right side of eternity with Him. You want Him to be your Lord, your Savior, your King, your very best friend.

PASTOR: If we ask the Father for anything that lines up with His will in the name of Jesus, He promises to give it to us. So I ask now in the name of Jesus, let us have a growing burning desire to seek Your will and walk in it in ways we can't even begin to imagine. Father let us hunger and thirst for the things you want from us, the things that will be pleasing in Your sight. Let Your love fill our hearts beyond measure. Let Your love flow out of us to others as You desire. Oh Father, let Your will be done in our lives, just as Your will is done in Heaven. We thank You for Jesus, for Your love, for being so patient and merciful. Help us, oh Father to be what You want us to be. Praise your Holy Name.

CHAPTER 4

THE WAY

BROTHER: This morning I was reading my devotional. This is out of Isaiah. Isaiah 55: 6-13 reads, *"Seek the Lord while He may be found, call upon Him while He is near. Let the wicked forsake his way, and the unrighteous man his thoughts; let him return to the Lord, and He will have mercy on him; and to our God, For He will abundantly pardon."*

"For My thoughts are not your thoughts, nor are your ways My ways," says the Lord. "For as the heavens are higher than the earth, so are My ways higher than your ways, And My thoughts than your thoughts."

"For as the rain comes down, and the snow from heaven, And do not return there, but water the earth, and make it bring forth the bud, that it may give seed to the sower and bread to the eater, so shall My word be that goes forth from My mouth; It shall not return to Me void, but it shall accomplish what I please, and it shall prosper in the thing for which I sent it."

"For you shall go out with joy, and be led out with peace; the mountains and the hills shall break forth into singing before you, and all the trees of the field shall clap their hands. "Instead of the thorn shall come up the cypress tree, and instead of the brier shall come up the myrtle tree; and it shall be to the Lord for a name, for an everlasting sign that shall not be cut off."

What got my attention this morning is our ways are not His ways. In our natural state we are not much like Him. If we do a big jump, from Isaiah to John 14:6-24 Jesus says it best. Would you read it?

PASTOR: Sure. John 14:6-24 reads:

"Jesus said to him, I am the way, the truth, and the life. No one comes to the Father except through Me."

"If you had known Me, you would have known My Father also; and from now on you know Him and have seen Him."

Philip said to Him, "Lord, show us the Father, and it is sufficient for us."

Jesus said to him, "Have I been with you so long, and yet you have not known Me, Philip? He who has seen Me has seen the Father; so how can you say, 'Show us the Father'?

"Do you not believe that I am in the Father, and the Father in Me? The words that I speak to you I do not speak on My own authority; but the Father who dwells in Me does the works."

"Believe Me that I am in the Father and the Father in Me, or else believe Me for the sake of the works themselves."

"Most assuredly, I say to you, he who believes in Me, the works that I do he will do also; and greater works than these he will do, because I go to My Father."

"And whatever you ask in My name, that I will do, that the Father may be glorified in the Son."

"If you ask anything in My name, I will do it."

"If you love Me, keep My commandments."

"And I will pray the Father, and He will give you another Helper, that He may abide with you forever – the Spirit of truth, whom the world cannot receive, because it neither sees Him nor knows Him; but you know Him, for He dwells with you and will be in you."

"I will not leave you orphans; I will come to you."

"A little while longer and the world will see Me no more, but you will see Me. Because I live, you will live also."

"At that day you will know that I am in My Father, and you in Me, and I in you."

"He who has My commandments and keeps them, it is he who loves Me. And he who loves Me will be loved by My Father, and I will love him and manifest Myself to him."

Judas (not Iscariot) said to Him, 'Lord, how is it that You will manifest Yourself to us, and not the world?'

Jesus answered and said to him, "If anyone loves Me, he will keep My word; and My Father will love him, and We will come to him and make Our home with him."

"He who does not love Me does not keep My words; and the word which you hear is not Mine but the Father's who sent Me."

BROTHER: That's deep.

PASTOR: God impressed this on me a while back. What He was doing in this passage, He was praying and giving instruction. Remember me telling you all the promises of God are yes and amen to those who are in Christ Jesus? That is what He is talking about here. If you keep His word, that's how you get in Christ Jesus. It's not a two minute prayer. It's a way of life, where you sacrifice your old life to have a new life in Him. You have given up being the lord of your life and allowed Him to rule and reign in your life because you have gone to the foot of the cross to receive His grace. It's only by His grace that we can keep His Word. It's not something we can do on our own or muster up in our own vigilance. It's something that He did. The only thing we can do, and most people don't understand it, most preachers don't preach it, is to walk in what He requires, in what He leads us to do. Jesus said, "If you love me, keep my Word." It says the same thing back here in Exodus 20:3-6, let me read this to you:

"You shall have no other gods before Me."

"You shall not make for yourself a carved image – any likeness of anything that is in heaven above, or that is in the earth beneath, or that is in the water under the earth; you shall not bow down to them nor serve them. For I, the Lord your God, am a jealous God, visiting the iniquity of the fathers upon the children to the third and fourth generations of those who hate Me, but showing mercy to thousands, to those who love Me and keep my commandments."

BROTHER: I think you're right. Most church people I know go back to their confession of Christ as Lord as their witness to being a Christian. I hope I'm not being judgmental, but a lot of them seem to lack a relationship with Jesus.

PASTOR: It's tough. Clearly, it is not our place to judge. Observation, maybe perception, can show us things sometimes. Let me drop back to where I left off in John, chapter 14, verses 25-31, Jesus is speaking:

"These things I have spoken to you while being present with you."

"But the Helper, the Holy Spirit, whom the Father will send in My Name, He will teach you all things, and bring to your remembrance all things that I said to you.

"Peace I leave with you, My peace I give to you; not as the world gives do I give to you. Let not your heart be troubled, neither let it be afraid.

You have heard Me say to you, 'I am going away and coming back to you.' If you loved Me, you would rejoice because I said, "I am going to the Father,' for My Father is greater than I.

"And now I have told you before it comes that when it does come to pass, you may believe.

"I will no longer talk much with you, for the ruler of this world is coming, and he has nothing in Me.

"But that the world may know that I love the Father, and as the Father gave Me commandment, so I do. Arise, let us go from here."

BROTHER: We could spend days talking about these verses, but it's crazy clear to me. Jesus loves us and He and the Father and the Holy Spirit want to have a tight relationship with each of us, very personal, much more personal than we can have with another human being.

PASTOR: You keep this up and I'm going to have you preaching.

There's joyful laughter.

BROTHER: We should probably pray about all this.

CHAPTER 5

THE TRUTH

The brother has been praying and reading the scriptures when he feels led to visit the pastor. When he gets to the pastors office he finds the pastor working on his computer with open books spread all over his desk and office. He hesitates for a moment and knocks on the open door. The pastor holds up his hand with one finger pointed to the ceiling. After a minute of typing the pastor turns around in his chair.

PASTOR: Good morning brother. Come on in. Let me move some of these books so you can sit. What's going on?

BROTHER: Is it ok if I talk to you for a minute? You look like you're deep into it.

PASTOR: Yea, come on in. What's up?

BROTHER: The Lord's been showing me something for a while and it's come to a head. I keep going back to the book of John, specifically John 14:6, which reads:

"Jesus said to him, I am the way, the truth, and the life. No one comes to the Father except through Me."

The word I'm focused on is truth. I can't seem to shake the idea that very few of us get to the truth. We're so distracted by the world we're in, the honest simple truth escapes us. Here Jesus says He is the truth. So, you tell me pastor, am I going wacko? I feel like not many people are getting this, some people in the church and definitely the world at large are so distracted and deceived they don't see the truth.

PASTOR: Well, to answer your question, yes, you are going wacko.

There's laughter.

PASTOR: Jesus tells us what the truth is. He tells us He is the truth. He tells us He is the way. He tells us He is life. I guess in essence everything outside of that is not the truth.

BROTHER: So maybe you've gone wacko too.

More laughter!

PASTOR: Quite frankly, yes.

BROTHER: We're both at a place where we wonder, what's going on?

PASTOR: Amazingly enough, the reason all these books are scattered around here, I'm in the midst of seeking a deeper understanding of the truth as it applies to the Christian walk. The grasp of the truth I have is that it is the written and spoken word of God as it is revealed by the Spirit of God to man. I believe walking in the truth opens the windows of heaven for a man to have dialogue with the One who created him. That's kind of where I'm at in my study.

When Moses comes down off the mountain with tablets of stone scribed on by the very finger of God, these were instructions for man to live by.

BROTHER: We know how that turned out. The people made a golden calf to worship, and if Moses hadn't pleaded on their behalf, I suppose on our behalf as well, we wouldn't exist. It doesn't seem like mankind changes much, we're still trying to worship things in spite of having a God that wants all our worship. When people are left to their own devices and the way of the world, which is controlled by the enemy, it leads them down a path of destruction where they're not doing what God wants. So you have God, who is the truth, Jesus says He is the truth, the Father is the truth, the Holy Spirit is the truth, this Word is the truth, and yet this world seems to control us, until we find the truth through God. It seems like we're living in a lost and dying world, where society, modern culture keep us from the truth with a barrage of distractions and distortions. I guess the simple thing He's shown me is that He is the truth. Everything that's not of Him is a false illusion created by falsehoods, lies and false hopes based on being socially, philosophically or even religiously correct.

PASTOR: True story. Go back to the Garden of Eden. Things were good, and God only made one stipulation on Adam and Eve. Genesis 2:16-17 tell us;

"And the Lord God commanded the man, saying, "Of every tree of the garden you may freely eat; "but of the tree of the knowledge of good and evil, you shall not eat, for in the day that you eat of it you shall surely die."

Along comes the serpent, who basically cons Eve into disobeying God. Everything changed for mankind on that day. The serpent is still active today, doing everything he can to con men and women into disobeying God. What do you think of that?

BROTHER: You're right. I give thanks to our Heavenly Father for loving us enough to make a way for us to see the truth through Jesus. It's hard to imagine how hard it must have been for the Jewish people to live all those centuries between the garden and the time of Jesus. They had a few good times, but the majority of the time they were distracted in a distorted reality manipulated by the serpent.

PASTOR: What do you think the world believes is the truth?

BROTHER: Part of what He has shown me is the truth the world believes is mostly a lie of one kind or another. I remember back in college days when we were listening to a lot of rock n roll and searching through countless philosophies we came to believe the government was corrupt and therefore it couldn't be trusted. We allowed ourselves to be manipulated by this perceived truth. I remember quoting part of scripture back then that was thrown around a lot of circles.

John 8:31-32 reads; *"Then Jesus said to those Jews who believed Him, "If you abide in My word, you are My disciples indeed. "And you shall know the truth, and the truth shall make you free."*

What we quoted was a rendition of verse 32. We'd say 'if you know the truth, the truth will set you free'. The truth we believed was a constantly changing truth. One day it was about corrupt politicians. The next day it was a belief about making enough money to be set free from work and society. That appealed to me for years, keeping my attention on money instead of God and Jesus. Of course when I was doing this I was completely ignoring verse 31. I didn't even know it at the time. Let me read that again, *"Then Jesus said to those Jews who believed Him, "If you abide in My word, you are My disciples indeed. "And you shall know the truth, and the truth shall make you free."*

PASTOR: It's interesting that I've been studying the concept of truth and you come here this morning basically doing the same thing. Jesus is the truth, and I don't think it's a big leap to find a deeper understanding of the truth in His words. He encourages us to pray, to fast, to keep the commandments, to continually seek Him, to give our hearts, our hopes, our lives over to His control. I believe we need to let Him truly be our Lord, our Savior, our guide through the help of the Holy Spirit. Life is a big circle of time and events. We're all in this circle, and yet each of us seems to be on an individual circle of sorts.

BROTHER: I agree. It all circles back to Him in countless ways. In the beginning, back in the garden, everything was true and good. Adam and Eve had a great thing. Then along comes the enemy, the serpent, full of lies and evil. He cons them into sinning and he's been conning people through the ages to sin. God has remained constant too, He loves us, and desires our love, our devotion. He wants to pour out wisdom on us. He wants us to find the only real truth there is and rest in it – rest in Him through Jesus.

PASTOR: The desire to sin seems to be more prevalent with every passing day in the world we live in. The boundaries are being pushed almost beyond belief in movies, on TV, on the internet. Our culture is obsessed with evil, with conspiracies, with sex, with violence, and filth of unimaginable darkness. It is socially correct to tolerate some or all of this, and at the same time it's not cool, if you will, to encourage people to seek God, to read the Bible, to simply read the ten commandments, to speak the name Jesus.

BROTHER: When I was reading this morning He took me back to 1 John. Let me borrow your Bible. This is 1 John, chapter 1;

"That which was from the beginning, which we have heard, which we have seen with our eyes, which we have looked upon, and our hands have handled, concerning the Word of life – the life was manifested, and we have seen, and bear witness, and declare to you that eternal life which was with the Father and was manifested to us – that which we have seen and heard we declare to you, that you also may have fellowship with us; and truly our fellowship is with the Father and with His Son Jesus Christ. And these things we write to you that your joy may be full."

"This is the message which we have heard from Him and declare to you, that God is light and in Him is no darkness at all. If we say that we have fellowship with Him, and walk in darkness, we lie and do not practice the truth. But if we walk in the light as He is in the light, we have fellowship with one another, and the blood of Jesus Christ His Son cleanses us from

all sin. If we say that we have no sin, we deceive ourselves, and the truth in not in us. If we confess our sins, He is faithful and just to forgive us our sins and to cleanse us from all unrighteousness. If we say that we have not sinned, we make Him a liar, and His word is not in us."

It's so powerful. I don't know how many times I've read this, but this morning it seems so undeniably true. The world culture is in an entirely different place, a place filled with darkness, hopelessness, unfulfilled hearts and lives, buzzing with sin.

PASTOR: That's right. The truth is available to walk in. If we live and walk in the light of truth we can abide in Him. Our joy may be full in Jesus. So how do we walk in the light of truth? Jesus made it so clear to me, He said if you love me, you will keep the commandments. I keep coming back to this and I guess it shouldn't be such a mystery that this has almost become a lost piece of the puzzle in a lot of churches. The Father gave guidelines to Adam and Eve. He gave the commandments to His people through Moses and Jesus reminds us of their importance.

BROTHER: Let me continue in 1 John, chapter 2:1-11 reads;

"My little children, these things I write to you, so that you may not sin. And if anyone sins, we have an Advocate with the Father, Jesus Christ the righteous. And He Himself is the propitiation for our sins, and not for ours only but also for the whole world."

"Now by this we know that we know Him, if we keep His commandments. He who says, "I know Him," and does not keep His commandments, is a liar, and the truth is not in him. But whoever keeps His word, truly the love of God is perfected in Him. He who says he abides in Him ought himself also to walk just as He walked."

"Brethren, I write no new commandment to you, but an old commandment which you have had from the beginning. The old commandment is the word which you heard from the beginning.

Again, a new commandment I write to you, which thing is true in Him and in you, because the darkness is passing away, and the true light is already shining. He who says he is in the light, and hates his brother, is in darkness until now. He who loves his brother abides in the light, and there is no cause for stumbling in him. But he who hates his brother is in darkness and walks in darkness, and does not know where he is going, because the darkness has blinded his eyes."

PASTOR: Hallelujah! We're finding some answers. I'm glad you came by.

BROTHER: Years ago I went to hear an evangelist speak and he said something profound to me. He said, "Get into the Word and let the Word get into you." So if these first two chapter of 1 John were read aloud in church and we pray for the Holy Spirit to help people receive this, how powerful would that be?

PASTOR: It could be amazing, if the time is right, and the Holy Spirit is in charge of it. It seems like most of the gospels and the epistles of John aren't popular to preach these days. If people are exposed to a lot of this, they can be confronted by the Holy Spirit with the truth of their spiritual condition. I wish I were wrong, but I suspect many people in church are there to feel good, sometimes having their ears tickled with positive pleasantries and half truths that convince them they are covered by grace, to the point of making it acceptable to sin and live in a way they choose.

BROTHER: Wow. That's rough. What's the answer?

PASTOR: Jesus is the answer. We need to return to our first love, Jesus. A lot of people came forward in church, or sat at home, prompted by a television program, and prayed a short prayer, accepting Jesus as their Savior, some even asked for forgiveness of their sins, and some proclaimed they'd repent, but

I fear many didn't move far past this prayer. Like we've talked today and the scriptures prove it out, being a Christian is a process, a life long process, a fabulous fulfilling process. Too often being a Christian is made out to be a simple option, like picking the color of a car or selecting the best place to vacation. We are saved by grace, but that grace can stay with us on a daily basis, and His power, through grace can actually help us to repent of our sins, to allow Him to change our hearts to become more and more like Him. He can help and enable us to change, to be healed from the inside out. I'm in the midst of this process every day and I strongly suspect you are too. Praise God!

Jesus left a lot of encouraging words for us. John 14:15-18 gives me a lot of hope. Jesus said; *"If you love Me, keep My commandments. And I will pray the Father, and He will give you another Helper, that He may abide with you forever – the Spirit of truth, whom the world cannot receive, because it neither sees Him nor knows Him; but you know Him, for He dwells with you and will be in you. I will not leave you orphans; I will come to you."*

BROTHER: Thank you pastor. And thank You Jesus.

PASTOR: Let's pray. Heavenly Father, we come to you in the name of your precious Son, Jesus, we thank you for blessing this time with Your Word and the sweet presence of the Holy Spirit. Please help us to convey these truths You've shown us in a way that is true and pleasing in Your sight. I pray in advance that You would begin to prepare the hearts of those that will receive Your truth. We thank You and Praise You in Your Sons holy name, Jesus. Amen.

CHAPTER 6

THE LIFE

The brother was at home quietly reading scripture, trying to better understand the word life, when there's a knock on the door. When he opens the door it's the pastor.

PASTOR: Morning brother. What's going on? Are you ready to go?

BROTHER: I guess I've missed something. Where are we going today?

PASTOR: We talked about going fishing. I wrote it on my calendar. Did you forget?

BROTHER: I guess so. I started studying the word life early this morning and lost track of time. Come on in. Maybe we can fish in the Word.

PASTOR: If you don't mind, tell me what's going on.

BROTHER: We've talked a lot about John 14:6 recently. We talked about the way and the truth and now I'm seeking some wisdom about the word life. We both know John 14:6.
  "Jesus said to him, 'I am the way, the truth, and the life. No one comes to the Father except through Me.'"
  I don't want to make it too simple and I don't want to make it too complicated. What do you think?

PASTOR: Life? What comes to my mind first is that life started in the beginning when God created everything.

The two sit down.

PASTOR: Can I borrow your Bible for a minute.

BROTHER: Gladly.

PASTOR: Genesis 2:7 reads, *"And the Lord God formed man of the dust of the ground, and breathed into his nostrils the breath of life; and the man became a living being."*
 So, the Lord God created life. Without Him nothing would exist, including us.

BROTHER: It's probably worth saying that Jesus is the person of God that created everything. Jesus is the creator of life itself.

PASTOR: It is worth noting. I know you've read this many times, but let me read this again, starting in John 1:1 and going through to verse 14:
 "In the beginning was the Word, and the Word was with God, and the Word was God. He was in the beginning with God. All things were made through Him, and without Him nothing was made that was made.
 In Him was life, and life was the light of men. And the light shines in the darkness, and the darkness did not comprehend it.
 There was a man sent from God, whose name was John. This man came for a witness, to bear witness of the Light, that all through him might believe. He was not that Light, but was sent to bear witness of that Light.
 That was the true Light which gives light to every man coming into the world. He was in the world, and world was made through Him, and world did not know Him. He came to His own and His own did not receive Him. But as many as received Him, to them He gave the right to become children of God, to those who believe in His name: who were born, not of blood, nor of the will of the flesh, nor of the will of man, but of God.
 And the Word became flesh and dwelt among us, and we beheld His glory, the glory as of the only begotten of the Father, full of grace and truth."

PASTOR: Two things seem obvious. There is no life without Him. And life is the opposite of death. If you are not spiritually alive you are spiritually dead. Even though we could be fishing today, I would much rather be telling everyone that will listen that Jesus is the way, the truth, and life itself, and no one comes to the Father except through Jesus. What does that mean? What does that mean to you?

BROTHER: In a very personal way, I spent much of my life not even thinking about God or Jesus. I just existed. I grew up and kind of bounced around in the world. When I came to know Jesus, some lights began to come on and I realized there is only one way to the Father, through Jesus, and I chose Him to be my Lord and Savior. I was born again. As time goes on there's more wisdom and understanding that come from Him. When I observe what's going on in the world, most of it is just like I was before I came to know Him, they don't realize their very existence comes from God, from Jesus. You said it well, they're spiritually dead, and spiritual life is only possible if Jesus is allowed into them and they are born again.

PASTOR: You bring up a profound point, in that in the early part of your life you didn't think about God or Jesus. Here's an amazing truth He's shown me. Even though the world at large doesn't seem to be thinking seriously about God or Jesus, He has been thinking about us from the very beginning and He will be thinking about us until the end. That's one of the awesome traits of God. You can live in spiritual death without Him, or you can have spiritual life with Him and in Him. And Him in you.

BROTHER: That's a good piece of wisdom to dwell on. A good catch if you will.

There's laughter.

BROTHER: He knew us at the point of conception when we were in our mothers' womb, and He already knows how we'll spend eternity, either in spiritual life or spiritual death. It is up to us. Fortunately, for you and me, He had mercy on us, and sought after us when we sought Him. He drew us to life through the saving blood of Jesus. Thank You Jesus. I know for me and I think from what you've said too, that was a huge awakening from what we came out of.

PASTOR: For some reason I'm remembering the conversation between Jesus and the Samaritan woman at the well. You remember it?

BROTHER: Yes, at least the highlights, where is that?

PASTOR: Look in John, I think chapter 4.

BROTHER: Yea, here it is. Let's see, John 4:7-26 says:
"A woman of Samaria came to draw water. Jesus said to her, 'Give Me a drink.' For His disciples had gone away into the city to buy food. Then the woman of Samaria said to Him, 'How is it that You, being a Jew, ask a drink from me, a Samaritan woman?' For Jews have no dealings with Samaritans.

Jesus answered and said to her, 'If you knew the gift of God, and who it is who says to you, 'Give Me a drink,' you would have asked Him, and He would have given you living water.'

The woman said to Him, "Sir, You have nothing to draw with, and the well is deep. Where then do you get that living water? Are You greater than our father Jacob, who gave us the well, and drank from it himself, as well as his sons and livestock?"

Jesus answered and said to her, "Whoever drinks of this water will thirst again, but whoever drinks of the water that I shall give him will never thirst. But the water that I shall give him will become in him a fountain of water springing up into everlasting life."

The woman said to Him, 'Sir, give me this water, that I may not thirst, nor come here to draw.'

Jesus said to her, 'Go call your husband, and come here.'

The woman answered and said, 'I have no husband.' Jesus said to her, 'You have well said, 'I have no husband, for you have had five husbands, and the one whom you now have is not your husband; in that you spoke truly."

The woman said to Him, 'Sir I perceive that You are a prophet. Our fathers worshiped on this mountain, and you Jews say that in Jerusalem is the place where one ought to worship.'

Jesus said to her, 'Woman, believe Me, the hour is coming when you will neither on this mountain, nor in Jerusalem, worship the Father. You worship what you do not know; we know what we worship, for salvation is of the Jews. But the hour is coming, and now is, when the true worshipers will worship the Father in spirit and truth; for the Father is seeking such to worship Him. God is Spirit, and those who worship Him must worship in spirit and truth.'

The woman said to Him, 'I know that Messiah is coming' (who is called Christ). When He comes, He will tell us all things.'

Jesus said to her, 'I who speak to you am He.'

PASTOR: It's an awesome story. It's an illustration of the spiritual life that comes only by Jesus. So many people walk outside of that life, so why is that? John 10:10 says:

"The thief does not come except to steal, and to kill, and to destroy. I have come that they may have life, and that they may have it more abundantly."

I believe Jesus was offering her that abundant life.

BROTHER: Essentially He's offering himself to her as a door to the Father, a door to eternal life, to spiritual life instead of the spiritual death she's existed in. If you go back to John 14:6.

"Jesus said to him, 'I am the way, the truth, and the life. No one comes to the Father except through Me.'"

Is it a leap to say that He's offered Himself to her?

PASTOR: Not really. Some might split hairs with you, but I'm not going to. He's responsible for physical life and He's responsible for spiritual life. We can't get there without him. Look at John 10, in fact read some of it aloud.

BROTHER: John 10:1-18 reads, and this is Jesus speaking,

"Most assuredly, I say to you, he who does not enter the sheepfold by the door, but climbs up some other way, the same is a thief and a robber. But he who enters by the door is the shepherd of the sheep. To him the doorkeeper opens, and the sheep hear his voice; and he calls his own sheep by name and leads them out. And when he brings out his own sheep, he goes before them; and the sheep follow him, for they know his voice. Yet they will by no means follow a stranger, but will flee from him, for they do not know the voice of strangers."

Jesus used this illustration, but they did not understand the things which He spoke to them.

Then Jesus said to them again, "Most assuredly I say to you, I am the door of the sheep. All who ever came before Me are thieves and robbers, but the sheep did not hear them. I am the door. If anyone enters by Me, he will be saved, and will go in and out and find pasture.

The thief does not come except to steal, and to kill, and to destroy. I have come that they may have life, and that they may have it more abundantly. I am the good shepherd. The good shepherd gives His life for the sheep.

But a hireling, he who is not the shepherd, one who does not own the sheep, sees the wolf coming and leaves the sheep and flees; and the wolf catches the sheep and scatters them. The hireling flees because he is a hireling and does not care about the sheep.

I am the good shepherd; and I know My sheep, and am known by My own. As the Father knows Me, even so I know the Father; and I lay down My life for the sheep. And other sheep I have which are not of this fold; them also I must bring, and they will hear My voice; and there will be one flock and one shepherd.

Therefore My Father loves Me, because I lay down My life that I may take it again. No one takes it from Me, but I lay it down of Myself. I have power to lay it down, and I have power to take it again. This command I have received from My Father."

I know that's a lot of scripture, but it's so clear and amazing to read it right now.

PASTOR: It is amazing. Let me read another scripture to you that goes along with it. Psalm 23 reads;

"The Lord is my shepherd. I shall not want. He makes me to lie down in green pastures; He leads me beside the still waters. He restores my soul; He leads me in the paths of righteousness For His name's sake. Yea, though I walk through the valley of the shadow of death, I will fear no evil. For You are with me; Your rod and Your staff, they comfort me. You prepare a table before me in the presence of my enemies; You anoint my head with oil; My cup runs over. Surely goodness and mercy shall follow me all the days of my life; And I will dwell in the house of the Lord Forever."

BROTHER: It just occurred to me that we are made in such a way that we all need a shepherd. All of us are being guided by one shepherd or another, whether it be Jesus, or some other shepherd like a politician, or a scientist, or an expert, or some worldly combination of characteristics.

PASTOR: Or it could be a religion, even a religion that claims to be Christian. Jesus is the only true shepherd. If we're not following Him in a very personal way, where we know Him and He knows us, we're going the wrong way, eventually into the fire of Hell if we don't change course and run to Him.

There's another element to Jesus that's worth talking about. I'm going back to the first chapter of John. John 1:17 says, *"For the law was given through Moses, but grace and truth came through Jesus Christ."*

So what does this mean? I think the law was given by God to show people how to live, how to be right with Him, but most couldn't live by it for one reason or another. In old testament times they could go to the temple in Jerusalem and make sacrifices, but most people probably didn't get far from the temple without breaking one or more of the commandments. Jesus, as John the Baptist put it, was the lamb of God. His willing sacrifice provided grace and truth, a new way to approach the father.

There's so many crazy things that went on when Jesus died on the cross. Luke 23:45 says;
   "Then the sun was darkened and the veil of the temple was torn in two."
So to me this is telling us that Jesus cancelled the whole animal blood sacrifice system. That veil was the entrance to the holy of holies, and Jesus replaced that access to God the Father with Himself. He is the life.

BROTHER: It occurred to me, you came here this morning to go trout fishing, but maybe as Jesus called upon Peter and his brother to leave their fishing boats and follow Him, to become fishers of men . . .

PASTOR: What, that we're fishers of men?

There's joyous laughter.

BROTHER: Maybe. Thank You Jesus.

PASTOR: One last scripture. Many think it's over used, but listen to John 3:16 with open ears. It reads;

"For God so loved the world that He gave His only begotten Son, that whoever believes in Him should not perish but have everlasting life."

CHAPTER 7

BORN AGAIN

BROTHER: Pastor, I'd like to talk to you about a friend of mine who is willing to talk about the Lord Jesus. I read a passage of scripture to him the other day, one we're both familiar with. Let me read John 3:1-21 to you;

"There was a man of the Pharisees named Nicodemus, a ruler of the Jews. This man came to Jesus by night and said to Him, "Rabbi, we know that You are a teacher from God; for no one can do these signs that You do unless God is with him."

Jesus answered and said to him, "Most assuredly, I say to you, unless one is born again, he cannot see the kingdom of God."

Nicodemus said to Him, "How can a man be born when he is old? Can he enter a second time into his mother's womb and be born?"

Jesus answered, "Most assuredly, I say to you, unless one is born of water and the Spirit, he cannot enter the kingdom of God. That which is born of flesh is flesh, and that which is born of the Spirit is spirit. Do not marvel that I said to you, "You must be born again. The wind blows where it wishes, and you hear the sound of it, but cannot tell where it comes from and where it goes. So is everyone who is born of the Spirit."

Nicodemus answered and said to Him, "How can these things be?"

Jesus answered and said to him, "Are you the teacher of Israel, and do not know these things? Most assuredly, I say to you, We speak what We know and testify what We have seen, and you do not receive Our witness. If I have told you earthly things and you do not believe, how will you believe if I tell you heavenly things? No one has ascended to heaven but He who came down from heaven, that is, the Son of Man who is in heaven. And as Moses lifted up the serpent in the wilderness, even so must the Son of Man be lifted up, that whoever believes in Him should not perish but have eternal life."

"For God so loved the world that He gave His only begotten Son, that whoever believes in Him should not perish but have everlasting life. For God did not send His Son into the world to condemn the world, but that the world through Him might be saved. He who believes in Him is not condemned; but he who does not believe is condemned already, because he has not believed in the name of the only begotten Son of God. And this is the condemnation, that the light has come into the world, and men loved darkness rather than light, because their deeds were evil. For everyone practicing evil hates the light and does not come to the light, lest his deeds should be exposed. But he who does the truth comes to the light, that his deeds may be clearly seen, that they have been done in God."

I read this to him and I stressed he's got to be born again before he can see the kingdom of God. There's not much point in trying to look into the kingdom of God unless you're born again, and then Jesus took it further by saying *"unless one is born of water and the Spirit, he cannot enter the kingdom of God."* **So what I'm trying to get across to him is that it's essential to be born again to see the kingdom of God, and to enter the kingdom of God. The only way to God is to be born again.**

PASTOR: You're absolutely right, a man needs to be born again to see and enter the kingdom of God. I think the fleshy side of man doesn't want to give up any of the pleasures of the flesh if that's what it means to be born again. Being born again is a new birth of the Spirit, which causes ones heart, spirit, and mind to begin a life long process of renewal. This renewal focus's on heavenly matters, love for the Father, love for Jesus, love for the Holy Spirit, learning to love all those around you as the Father wants us to love them. To someone who is not born again, seeking to do the will of our Heavenly Father is alien to them.

BROTHER: The essential thing I'm stressing to this guy is that you must be born again to see the kingdom of God and you must be born again to enter the kingdom of God. There is no other way to God, no shortcuts or alternate paths, other than believing that Jesus Christ is the only begotten Son of God, sent as a willing sacrifice for each of us personally. He died on the cross as the perfect blood sacrifice for each of us. One of the most crystal clear scriptures that speaks of this is 2 Corinthians 5:17;

"Therefore, if anyone is in Christ, he is a new creation; old things have passed away; behold all things have become new."

To me this makes it clear that if we are born again we're in a new life. It's different than the life we were born into in the flesh and in my case grew up in. Nicodemus was apparently a very religious man, and yet he was not born again. There was no change in his life, he was not born again spiritually.

PASTOR: Let me read Proverbs 14:12, it says, *"There is a way that seems right to man, but its end is the way of death."*

To the man who is not born again, he finds a way to live in this world that is outside the kingdom of God. The death spoken of here is an eternal death. I pray that people would come to understand their need of a Savior. Death outside of Jesus is eternal death, or as it's described in some places, eternal torment or eternal damnation. If people could somehow get a hold of this truth you'd think millions would rush to Jesus.

BROTHER: Exactly.

PASTOR: There are things that try to hold them where they're at. Those things are the lies of the devil. These things can make a person believe that he is ok, even good in some cases, but without Jesus we're condemned as the scripture puts it. The world has a hold on us until we are born again. Let me read something else from the old testament. In the end of

Ecclesiastes, chapter 12:13-14 it says, *"Let us hear the conclusion of the whole matter:*

Fear God and keep His commandments, For this is man's all. For God will bring every work into judgment. Including every secret thing, whether good or evil."

I think I've told you before, God knows all about us. He knows if we've found satisfaction or some kind of contentment in this worldly life and we're trying to convince ourselves that we can be fine without Him.

BROTHER: It occurred to me a while back that God has made each of us with an empty place in our heart that only He can fill. Everyone that I know tries to fill this empty place or void with something, relationships, power, alcohol, drugs, or even seemingly harmless hobbies, like sports, hunting or fishing, just to mention a few.

PASTOR: True story. Hopefully with this friend of yours, he will have his eyes opened to the fact that being born again is the only option to starting a new life with Jesus, a new eternal life that saves him from his own devices and the lies of the enemy.

BROTHER: I've thought a lot about the conversation between Jesus and Nicodemus. There are a lot of levels to it. I suspect I don't see them all, but it appears Nicodemus came to Jesus in some kind of quest to figure out exactly who Jesus was. It's remarkable to me that after Nicodemus seems to flatter Jesus, Jesus almost ignores what was said and repeatedly tells him that he must be born again. And from Nicodemus's response it appears that he's clueless about understanding what Jesus is telling him.

PASTOR: We've talked a lot about being born again, but how and why does anyone reach a point where they want to be born again?

BROTHER: You tell me pastor.

PASTOR: I'll start with Isaiah 59:1-2:
"Behold, the Lord's hand is not shortened, that it cannot save; nor His ear heavy, that it cannot hear. But your iniquities have separated you from God; and your sins have hidden His face from you, so that He will not hear."
There's that word many hate to preach about and many don't want to hear – sin, but it is part of the deal. Paul says it very clearly. Romans 3:23 says, *"For all have sinned and fall short of the glory of God."*
Paul goes on in Romans 6:23 to say, *"For the wages of sin is death, but the gift of God is eternal life in Christ Jesus our Lord."*
I believe it is necessary for a person to realize, all have sinned and the wages of sin is death. Almost all people realize they have committed a sin of some sort.

BROTHER: I agree, now what.

PASTOR: This is part of what I love to share. There is good news! Hallelujah! 1 Timothy 2:5 says, *'For there is one God and one Mediator between God and men, the Man Christ Jesus"*
1 Peter 3:18 says, *"For Christ also suffered once for sins, the just for the unjust, that He might bring us to God, being put to death in the flesh but made alive by the Spirit"*
Romans 5:8 says, *"But God demonstrates His own love toward us, in that while we were still sinners, Christ died for us."*
It still amazes me, every time it comes to mind, how much God the Father loves us, much more that we can comprehend, I'm sure.

BROTHER: Amen brother.

PASTOR: The real place of being born again is when you confess that you're a sinner and believe, and I mean truly believe that Jesus went to the cross as a sacrifice for the sins of the world, which include mine, yours and your friends. On top of this one needs to confess with his mouth that Jesus Christ is Lord, and by this I mean a person needs to ask and receive Jesus as their personal Lord and Savior. This is the point where you begin a new life with Jesus, allowing the Holy Spirit to lead you into all righteousness and turning the direction of your life over to Him. For most of us it is a recognizable change in our hearts and minds.

Jesus gives a lot of truly amazing guidance and advice in the gospels. Matthew 6:33 says, *"But seek first the kingdom of God and His righteousness, and all things shall be added to you."*

The word seek here could better be translated to seek, and continue to seek, and seek and seek, and then keep seeking. I believe Jesus wants our constant attention. We can live in Christ.

BROTHER: Can I pray, and you can add to it if need be?

PASTOR: Go ahead.

BROTHER: We come to You Heavenly Father to ask for help. Help me Lord to say the right words so my friend can be born again. I ask You to pour out the Holy Spirit on him in such a way that the truth will be undeniable to him. I know that You love all of us and that you want my friend to be saved by the gift that you gave for all of us, Your Only Begotten Son Jesus. Oh Father, let your will be done in this matter, just as Your will is done in heaven. Thank You Father for Jesus. Thank You for the Holy Spirit. Again I ask, let the Holy Spirit draw my friends heart to You. I ask these things in the name of Jesus. Amen.

PASTOR: Amen.

CHAPTER 8

JESUS IS LORD AND SAVIOR

BROTHER: Pastor, I've got great news, my friend got saved last night.

PASTOR: Hallelujah! Praise You Heavenly Father! Praise You Jesus! Tell me about it.

BROTHER: He told me he kept reading the third chapter of John, that amazing conversation between Nicodemus and Jesus, and he asked God to show him the truth. He told me he knew in his heart that he needed to be born again. We prayed together and the presence of the Holy Spirit swept over us. It was amazing. He's yearning to know more about Jesus.

PASTOR: Thank you Jesus. What did you tell him?

BROTHER: Scriptures poured out of me. First, I felt led to quote Matthew 6:33, where Jesus said, *"But seek first the kingdom of God and His righteousness, and all these things shall be added to you."* Then came Matthew 11:28-30 where Jesus said, *"Come to Me, all you who labor and are heavy laden, and I will give you rest. Take My yoke upon you and learn from Me, for I am gentle and lowly in heart, and you will find rest for your souls."*
"For My yoke is easy and My burden is light."

PASTOR: Sounds good. Did he receive the scriptures?

BROTHER: I think so. I told him to do everything he could to receive the love Jesus has for him. I encouraged him to pray as much as possible, to read the gospels, Matthew, Mark, Luke and John. I hope I did what Jesus wanted me to do. I did warn him that the enemy would probably mess with him and encouraged him to keep seeking Jesus and all the love and truth and life that's now available to him.

PASTOR: Obviously, we need to keep him in our prayers. I'll be praying for a hedge of protection around him and that the Holy Spirit will continue to draw him into the love and truth of the Heavenly Father through Jesus. The words of Jesus in the gospels are where it's at for a new believer. So much circles around Jesus.

BROTHER: A light came on at one point last night. I remember reading Matthew 7:13-14 to him, where Jesus said, *"Enter by the narrow gate; for wide is the gate and broad is the way that leads to destruction, and there are many who go in by it."*

"Because narrow is the gate and difficult is the way which leads to life; and there are few who find it."

PASTOR: That scripture has been in a lot of our conversations lately.

BROTHER: Yes, and last night I put it together with John 14:6, where Jesus said, *"I am the way, the truth, and the life. No one comes to the Father except through Me."*

I encouraged him to allow the truth of the words of Jesus to fill his heart and mind. Jesus truly is the only way to the Father. The wisest thing we can do is get as close to Jesus as possible, so close that we continue to grow in our awe and love and understanding of Him. He is the Messiah, the King of kings, the Lord of lords.

PASTOR: Amen brother. In the book of Revelation 1:11, Jesus told John and all of us, *"I am the Alpha and the Omega, the First and the Last."* I'm not sure how much we will come to know Jesus in this earthly state, but I know the depths of who He is are beyond measure." You and I both know the relationship we have with Him continues to grow and expand. For some though, they get stalled or choose to limit their relationship. I might be getting off subject a little, but let me share something that happened to me early on and you can decide whether it's worth sharing with your friend.

I started attending a church shortly after I got saved and someone there volunteered me to go out with others and visit people who had visited the church. I was out one night with an older couple and their daughter. We were sitting in their car in the parking lot after praying together. I started talking about some other church members, actually more like complaining and the couples daughter spoke up when I was finished.

She read Hebrews 12:1-2 to me, *"Therefore we also, since we are surrounded by so great a cloud of witnesses, let us lay aside every weight, and the sin which so easily ensnares us, and let us run with endurance the race that is set before us, looking unto Jesus, the author and finisher of our faith."*

Part of that pierced my heart, the part where it says, *looking unto Jesus, the author and finisher of our faith."*

I realized how easy it is to take our eyes off Jesus and get distracted to the point of ridiculousness. I give thanks to Jesus for continuing to bring me back to His will and not mine.

BROTHER: That's good pastor. What's your advice now?

PASTOR: Continue to pray for him and with him as the Spirit leads you. When the time is right, encourage him to be baptized. The end of Matthew, 28:18-20 says:

And Jesus came and spoke to them saying, *"All authority has been given to Me in heaven and on earth. Go therefore and make disciples of all the nations, baptizing them in the name of the Father and the Son and the Holy Spirit, teaching them to observe all things that I have commanded you; and lo, I am with you always, even to the end of the age."*

BROTHER: Ok. I'll be prayerful about it.

PASTOR: You know there's more. Trust in the Father, in Jesus, and the Holy Spirit to lead you in all things. Jesus is more than capable. I think you know that.

BROTHER: I'll do my best. Keep me in your prayers. I don't want to mess this up.

PASTOR: I will my brother. I want to share something with you that's on my heart. I'm concerned that many in the church in general, even some in our church have settled for a shallow understanding of what Jesus wants them to do. He does not want any of us to feel like we've reached a place of completion or contentment in our walk with Him. I hope I'm not preaching to the choir, as some say, but let me read some often overlooked verses to you, Jesus says in Matthew 5:17-19;

"Do not think that I came to destroy the Law or the Prophets. I did not come to destroy but to fulfill."

"For assuredly, I say to you, till heaven and earth pass away, one jot or one tittle will by no means pass from the law till all is fulfilled."

"Whoever therefore breaks one of the least of these commandments, and teaches men so, shall be called least in the kingdom of heaven; but whoever does and teaches them, he shall be called great in the kingdom of heaven."

I know some will say this is too hard, and some will teach the law ended when Jesus died on the cross, but I have to say Jesus is the ultimate authority.

BROTHER: I agree with that.

PASTOR: Do you know the commandments by heart?

BROTHER: No.

PASTOR: Don't feel bad. Let me read this to you, because I've found myself repeatedly reading them.

Exodus 20:1-17 says:

And God spoke all these words, saying:

"I am the LORD your God, who brought you out of the land of Egypt, out of the house of bondage."

"You shall have no other gods before Me."

"You shall not make for yourself a carved image – any likeness of anything that is in heaven above, or that is in the earth beneath, or that is in the water under the earth; you shall not bow down to them nor serve them. For I, the LORD your God, am a jealous God, visiting the iniquity of the fathers upon the children to the third and fourth generations of those who hate Me, but showing mercy to thousands, to those who love Me and keep My commandments."

"You shall not take the name of the LORD your God in vain, for the LORD will not hold him guiltless who takes His name in vain."

"Remember the Sabbath day, to keep it holy. Six days you shall labor and do all your work, but the seventh day is the Sabbath of the LORD your God. In it you shall do no work; you nor your son, nor your daughter, nor your male servant, nor your female servant, nor your cattle, nor your stranger who is within your gates. For in six days the LORD made the heavens and the earth, the sea, and all that is in them, and rested the seventh day. Therefore the LORD blessed the Sabbath day and hallowed it."

"Honor your father and your mother, that your days may be long upon the land which the LORD your God is giving you."

"You shall not murder."

"You shall not commit adultery."

"You shall not steal."

"You shall not bear false witness against your neighbor."

"You shall not covet your neighbor's house; you shall not covet your neighbor's wife, nor his male servant, nor his female servant, nor his ox, nor his donkey, nor anything that is your neighbor's."

PASTOR: I know it's a lot of stuff to consider and understand.

BROTHER: Wow! You're right about that.

PASTOR: In my lifetime I've seen the commandments removed from schools and most public buildings. Jesus helped us out though, here's what Matthew 22:34-40 says:

> *But when the Pharisees heard that He had silenced the Sadducees, they gathered together. Then one of them, a lawyer, asked Him a question, testing Him, and saying, "Teacher, which is the great commandment in the law?"*
>
> *Jesus said to him, "You shall love the LORD your God with all your heart, with all your soul, and with all your mind. This is the first and great commandment. And the second is like it: You shall love your neighbor as yourself."*

BROTHER: That's definitely more concise.

PASTOR: In all these matters I believe we should invite the Holy Spirit to examine our hearts and minds and give us clear understanding of what's right and what's not. If you find yourself trying to justify behavior or attitudes that are questionable it's often better to seek God's will, not your own. It's not as complicated as we sometimes make it. Remember the way the serpent tricked Eve in the garden? He's working overtime to mess with us now.

BROTHER: I appreciate your help. Any last thoughts before I get out of here?

PASTOR: Encourage your friend as you have been. Keep him in constant prayer. Help him to understand that being a Christian is an amazing gift that grows with time. Jesus remains the way, the only way and as He said, *"narrow is the gate and difficult is the way which leads to life, and there are few who find it."*

CHAPTER 9

DAD AND SON

SON: Dad I know you were a young man when you got saved, but you never really told me how it came about.

DAD: It is a long story.

SON: I've got time if you do.

DAD: My parents weren't regular church goers. My mom took us a few times, but I don't remember my dad ever going. My sister and I used to go sporadically to different churches with friends, but we didn't stick with any of them. I guess as a kid I was most often in a play mode. I didn't pay much attention to the teaching or the preaching.

SON: So you never really heard about Jesus?

DAD: I probably heard the name. I guess I wasn't mature enough to really pay attention. When I was fifteen or so I went on a trip with my grandparents, my moms' parents, to Arizona. We lived in California at the time and we were close to my grandparents. They loved to travel and I was often invited to travel with them. My dads' parents lived in Arizona and I rarely got to see them. In any event, one set of grandparents dropped me off for a few days to spent time with the other set of grandparents. They were living on the grounds of the arboretum outside Superior, Arizona. It was an amazing place. Grandpa Doss was a groundskeeper there. I hung out with Grandpa part of the time while he worked.

One afternoon I stayed in the house with Grandma Doss after lunch. She was a sweet lady. All of us grandkids loved her and she was one of those people that loved you in a way that made you feel special. I still miss her and she's been gone for 40 years. Sorry, didn't mean to get sidetracked.

SON: That's OK.

DAD: So we're sitting around talking and she asks me something like, "Have you ever heard about Jesus?"

I was honest with her, I'd heard the name, but that's about all.

She asked me if she could tell me about Him and I had no objections. I know she quoted some scriptures. I can't tell you which ones, but she explained Jesus to me in a simple way that made perfect sense to me. The essence of what she told me is that Jesus is the only Son of God the Father and that He was born to save all of us, because of Gods' love for us. She explained that everyone has sinned, and the only remedy for our sin is to accept what Jesus did on our behalf when he was crucified on the cross. I know now the Holy Spirit was all over us. Her explanation was crystal clear to me at the time.

Then she asked me, "Would you accept Jesus Christ as your personal savior?"

I was in some weird state of shock I guess. After thinking about it for a minute or two, I told her no, I was not ready to do anything like that yet.

SON: So what did she say?

DAD: I don't really remember. I think she just dropped it. I suspect she was disappointed, but I believe she spent a lot of time in prayer for her kids and grandkids. Looking back on it I can't give you a good reason for my decision, other than some strange sense of wanting freedom.

SON: Did you ever talk to her again about it?

DAD: I don't think so. I saw her quite a few times before she passed, but there were always a lot of family around.

SON: What happened next?

DAD: You've heard me talk about being in the Boy Scouts.

SON: Yea, a few times.

DAD: Bill Colbert was my best friend in Boy Scouts. We went to high school together and we got to be close. I think we were juniors in high school when Bill started dating a girl who happened to be the daughter of a preacher. So Bill starts going to church with her and he gets saved. And then the two of them start talking to me about Jesus. I still wasn't interested, so we saw less and less of each other because he was constantly with her.

SON: You can't blame him for that.

DAD: So the summer between our junior and senior years Bill and I decided we'd go to the Boy Scout summer camp one last time and try to push ahead with getting our eagle scout awards. We shared a two man tent at camp that had a wood floor. It was a lot of fun, but pretty cramped quarters. Bill talked to me about Jesus a lot and one night I really lost my cool. I decided that I wasn't really convinced of the existence of God. I'm ashamed of this now, but one night Bill wouldn't let up. I confessed to him that I wasn't sure there is a God. I went outside the tent in the dark and held my hands up in the air. "If you're really there God I ask you to strike me with lightning." I glanced at Bill. He was cringing. Nothing happened. I repeated myself and still nothing happened. Somehow I felt I proved my point, and Bill didn't talk to me about Jesus for a while.

SON: I can't believe you did that.

DAD: I can't believe in some ways I got away with it. It was one of the dumbest things I've ever done. Thank God for his patience with me.

SON: So then what happened?

DAD: Bill and I got our eagle scout awards in our senior year of high school. Bill and I drifted apart. He went in the Air Force out of high school and I headed to college. I went off the deep end the summer out of high school. I got a pretty good paying job when I was still in high school. I got an apartment with some friends and my life became a non stop party. I went to college classes, worked almost full time and partied in between. It was crazy. Almost everyone I worked with and the friends I had were all into the party scene. One day I'm actually alone in the house we were renting, studying for a test, when there's a knock on the door. I ignored it for a while, but the third round of knocking got me up. I opened the door and it was a guy I'd known from grammar school. I'd had his sister in a lot of classes. I can't even remember his name now. He wanted to come in and talk to me about Jesus. For some reason I relented, and he let me have it for probably an hour. What he told me was the same stuff I'd heard from my grandma and Bill Colbert, but he told me about Hell too, and made me wonder. He told me he was a Jesus freak and he wanted everyone else to become one too. I pretty much blew him off, but I couldn't help wondering if there was something to all this Jesus stuff. You really want to hear all this?

SON: Yea, keep going.

DAD: Life started flying by. I eventually grew out of most of the party life. I decided the best thing for me was to make enough money to be free of a job. I became obsessed with working, sometimes two or three jobs. College seemed like a waste of time. I bought several pieces of property and kept pushing forward. There were a couple girlfriends, but nothing lasted. Then your mom got a job with the company I worked for. We started dating and after about six months we decided to get married. She was brought up Catholic and we thought it would be cool to get married outside by a priest. She made an appointment for us with a priest. It didn't go well at all.

SON: What happened?

DAD: The priest told me we could not be married unless I became a Catholic. One of my college roommates became a Catholic so he could get married. It was a joke. He and I use to get half drunk before he'd go to his conversion classes. I told the priest I wasn't having any of it. He basically told your mom and I our marriage would be cursed. She was really upset and I basically told him in to buzz off.

We eventually got married by a pastor that had married some of our friends. He was really a nice guy, and honestly counseled us about how to treat each other in our marriage. He said something like, "If you put the other one ahead of yourself as much as possible, you'll have a good marriage." It was a practical example of the Golden Rule. It was good and it stuck with both of us.

SON: Did Mom go the church then?

DAD: Not really. I changed jobs several times after we got married, always to make more money. One guy I worked for said he was a Christian, but honestly he turned out to be a pretty rotten guy. In some ways it turned me off to Christians and church in general.

SON: What went on to turn you toward God?

DAD: When you were born it started changing me and your mom. You've heard the story. You were born with problems and the Doctor told me you probably only had a 1 in 10 chance of making it. Your mom and I turned to God in our own ways. I probably tried to make some kind of a deal with Him. Your mom never stopped believing in God since she was a child. You've heard the story, you spent the first 3 months of your life in a hospital, and you were a sick little guy for a long time. All the doctors, nurses, and a lot of our friends and family called you a miracle baby.

Somewhere in the midst of all that my Aunt Janice from Arizona sent me a Christian book about raising children and a little tract, "Steps to Peace With God". She called me occasionally and asked me if I'd read the book and the tract. Eventually I did and the tract caused me to honestly question – Is there really a God? Aunt Janice's daughter Lisa started calling me too and telling me about how Jesus was changing her life. Both of them told me they'd be praying for me.

There's a long moment of silence.

SON: So keep going.

DAD: Weird circumstances happened. I managed to pay our house off and we had a little income coming in. I got laid off and your mom got a job. I spent my days working on the house, watching you and wondering what was next. I decided one day that I needed to figure out if God is for real or not. I had a Bible my grandparents gave me as a child. I decided to read through it and try to figure out if God is real. I began praying in a way, I asked God to show me if He is real or not. It took me about a week to read through the Bible. I started watching a lot of Christian TV and kept going over the tract Aunt Janice sent me.

The more I studied and prayed the more I began to believe the possibility of Gods existence.

SON: What finally made you get saved?

DAD: Without a doubt it was the Holy Spirit, and probably a lot of prayers over the years from family and friends. I kept reading the gospels and I remember Jesus saying something like, the gospel is so simple, even a little child can understand it. So as I repeatedly read that tract, "Steps to Peace With God". It became simple for me. I certainly didn't have peace with God. I almost memorized John 3:16, "For God so loved the world that he gave his one and only Son, that whoever believes in him shall not perish but have eternal life." I began to get part of it and it was amazing to me that God loved us, me in particular. I didn't have a problem realizing I was a sinner, maybe one of the worst ones ever. I remember reading Romans 3:23, "For all have sinned and fall short of the glory of God." This was a revelation to me in some ways, I never really thought about everyone being sinners. Romans 6:23 expanded my understanding, "For the wages of sin is death, but the gift of God is eternal life in Christ Jesus our Lord."

"Let me find the tract." Here it is. I can't remember all the scriptures, but each one began to come alive for me. Let me read these to you.

"For there is one God and one mediator between God and men, the man Christ Jesus." 1 Timothy 2:5

"For Christ died for sins once for all, the righteous for the unrighteous, to bring you to God." 1 Peter 3:18

"But God demonstrates his own love for us in this: While we were still sinners, Christ died for us." Romans 5:8

SON: Powerful verses.

DAD: There's a few more.

"Here I am! I stand at the door and knock. If anyone hears my voice and opens the door, I will come in and eat with him and he with me." Revelation 3:20

"Yet to all who received him, to those who believed in his name, he gave the right to become children of God." John 1:12

"That if you confess with your mouth, 'Jesus is Lord,' and believe in your heart that God raised him from the dead, you will be saved." Romans 10:9

A lot of people think it's corny, but I got down on my knees and I prayed the prayer in the back:

Dear Lord Jesus,
 I know that I am a sinner and need Your forgiveness. I believe that You died for my sins. I want to turn from my sins. I now invite You to come into my heart and life. I want to trust and follow You as Lord and Savior.

SON: So what happened? Did it hit you quick?

DAD: I was truly born again. I read the Bible a lot. I began to focus on the gospels, particularly Matthew and John. All of the sudden the scriptures that I could hardly read before, came alive to me. I felt my eyes were opened like never before. A lot of things began to make sense to me. I wanted to live for Jesus and I couldn't help wanting to share what I'd discovered with everyone around me. Almost all of my friends and family didn't really want to be around me. I overheard one family member, thinking I was out of hearing distance, refer to me as the preacher. It's funny now. It was a blessing to me.

SON: Wow. Who was that?

DAD: It doesn't matter. It changed my life. Your Mom wasn't thrilled with me. I was relentless with her. I felt our marriage wasn't going to make it, for a lot of reasons. I decided if we moved to a new setting we might have a chance. I convinced your Mom to go along with me. A few months later we put our house up for sale and I prayed, I asked God to show me by how the house sale worked out. We got a cash offer the second day it was on the market, and I took that as an affirmation. A lot of stuff went on, but the short version is, we moved from Chico, California to Globe, Arizona. We began going to church with Aunt Janice and God really moved on our lives. The Pastor and his wife became almost immediate friends with us. The Pastors wife had been brought up Catholic like your Mom. We were probably only there a couple months when your Mom got saved. Both of us were baptized in that church. It did not make either of us perfect, but we became united in our spirits with Jesus in a way neither of us could have imagined. It was great, what marriage is supposed to be like.

We witnessed to a lot of people over the years, strangers, friends and family. We saw a lot of people get saved. We learned to turn all our decisions over to the Lord in prayer. Outside of Jesus your Mom became my best friend. We found ourselves in the midst of churches falling apart and in the midst of some services where the Holy Spirit was so sweet and heavy that we couldn't help crying. Jesus stayed in the center of our lives through everything. After your Mom became disabled and slowly lived through increasing levels of pain, we still looked to Jesus for answers. It's hard not to get emotional when I dwell on your Mom. I miss her presence every day.

SON: It's ok Dad.

DAD: Your Mom eventually reached a point where she began praying for miraculous healing or that He'd take her home. At first it really upset me, but I knew how much she was hurting. It wasn't getting any better. I agreed to pray with her, I even asked that He'd take both of us home together. It's remarkable now to think back on all the books about Heaven that she and I read the last year of her life.

There's a pause and teary eyes.

SON: I know it's hard.

DAD: I found her that morning laying in bed with a paper plate in her lap with two oatmeal cookies on it. She looked like she'd just fallen asleep. I tried to wake her, but she was gone. I called the emergency people, then you, and then our close friends. I couldn't stop crying for hours. I began crying out to my Heavenly Father and Jesus to help me. He did. An indescribable peace came over me and I knew she was with God.

SON: So you're confident she's in Heaven?

DAD: Yes I am. MY TIME IN HEAVEN, by Richard Sigmund, is a book your Mom and I both read before her passing. Both of us found it to be amazing and encouraging. I had a lot of peace about her going to heaven. She accepted Jesus as her Lord and Savior years ago with all her heart. Obviously that didn't make her perfect, but it did make her saved when she wholeheartedly invited Jesus into her heart to rule and reign as her Lord.

About a month after she passed I woke up on a Saturday and felt a dark cloud of depression surrounding me like I've never experienced. I got up and started praying for relief. As I prayed I felt led to start reading MY TIME IN HEAVEN.

As I began reading, specifically pages 16 through 18, I got a vision of you Mom and her arrival in Heaven. I can still see this clearly now, and it's given me unspeakable peace and comfort when I'm feeling the loss of my wife and best friend.

I saw your Mom coming out of a cloud similar to what's described in the book. When I first saw her she was as she left earth, frail, stooped over and older looking than her years. In an instant she straightened up, and her appearance transformed back to her mid twenties, her hair was long and dark, she was beaming with beauty and the smile on her face exuded peace and love. She was made whole, without anymore pain or suffering by a God that loves each of us more than we can even begin to imagine.

I know God is preparing me for eternity. I would rather be in heaven now with Jesus and your Mom and the rest of our family and friends that are there. Your Mom and I spent a lot of time over the last thirty some years praying for all our family and friends. We continually asked God to draw everyone to a true understanding of His love for each of us. He does love everyone and wants to have a personal relationship with each individual. His desire, according to the Bible, is that none should perish, no not one. He wants all of us to spend eternity in heaven with Him.

SON: He's keeping you here for a reason or reasons. I love you Dad.

DAD: I love you too Son, with all my heart. Don't ever forget that Jesus loves you much more than you can imagine.

Made in United States
Orlando, FL
16 December 2021